seeds

SCRIPTURE PRAYERS
FOR YOUR FAMILY

Carrie D. Rogers

i

The LORD *is near to all who call on him, to all who call on him in truth.*

Psalm 145:1

TABLE OF CONTENTS

INTRODUCTION

When you plant a seed, you bury it deep in the dirt. It's an investment in the soil. Tiny and fragile, change comes slowly. In due season, with water, light and patience, you reap what you sow. The one who does the planting only waits and watches. It is God who makes all things grow.

The same is true with prayer. When we pray, we sow a seed of faith deep into the heart of God. This prayer, this tiny seed grounded in the promises of God, is an investment of eternal value. But the sower, the one who prays, only waits and watches. It is God who makes all things grow.

Welcome to *Seeds*, a little book of scripture prayers for you and your family. The prayers written in this book are my seeds sown over and over again on behalf of my people, the ones I hold most dear. They are an investment made over time—words offered and released to the One who makes all things grow. These prayers are for them *and* for me. God continues to use them to change us all.

The prayers in this book are broken up into three categories:

- · Prayers for your man
- · Prayers for your littles
- · Prayers for you

They cover a variety of topics specific to each category. The list of topics, arranged in no particular order, is in no way a comprehensive list. It's my prayer that these words will simply become a starting place of prayer for you.

Below each prayer is space for you to continue your conversation with God—a place to make the prayer specific and personal to your family. You may want to use those lines to jot down the date of your request or specific answers as they come. Use the space provided to make these prayers your own.

I pray that these little seeds are a blessing to you and your family. May God use these words to bolster your faith, strengthen your people and glorify the name of our good and faithful God for generations to come.

FOR YOUR MAN

WORK

Father, thank you for the work you have provided for _(your husband's name)_ through his job. May your favor rest upon him as you establish the work of his hands. Make him effective and productive in his daily tasks at work. I pray that he would find fulfillment, satisfaction and success in the work you have provided for him, but that ultimately he would only feel complete satisfaction in you. Thank you for providing for our family through my husband's job.

> _May the favor of the Lord our God rest upon us;_
> _establish the work of our hands for us—_
> _yes, establish the work of our hands._
> _Psalm 90:17_

_____

_____

_____

_____

_____

PURPOSE

Lord, thank you that you have called _(your husband's name)_ to a life of purpose. I pray that you may count him worthy of the life to which you have called him. Continue to mold him and make him into the man you have created him to be. By your power, fulfill every good work and faithful deed in him today. If he is struggling with his purpose, reveal it to him in a fresh way, I pray.

With this in mind, we constantly pray for you, that our God may count you worthy of his calling, and that by his power he may fulfill every good purpose of yours and every act prompted by your faith.
2 Thessalonians 1:11

_____

_____

_____

_____

_____

TEMPTATIONS

Father, I pray against any temptations that may come before my husband. I pray that he would literally hate what is evil and cling to what is good. Thank you for the truth that you reveal to us through your Word. Please guard my husband's mind from being lured by Satan's lies by drawing him toward Truth. Give _(your husband's name)_ the strength and courage to flee from temptations, to deny the desires of his flesh and to walk in the power of the Spirit.

Hate what is evil; cling to what is good.
Romans 12:9

_____

_____

_____

_____

_____

MIND

Lord, I pray that you would protect (*your husband's name*)'s mind today. Teach him how to take each thought captive to make it obedient to you. Please give him the desire to fill his mind with your Word so that he can stand in your truth. Thank you that when he turns his thoughts towards you, you promise to guard his heart and mind with a peace beyond all understanding.

We demolish arguments and every pretension that sets itself up against the knowledge of God, and we take captive every thought to make it obedient to Christ.
2 Corinthians 10:5

_____

_____

_____

_____

_____

WISDOM

Father God, I pray that (*your husband's name*) would be a man of wisdom. Where he is lacking in wisdom, grow in him the discipline to seek you, for you promise to give generously to all without finding fault. I pray that my husband's choices would reflect your character and the truth found in Your Word. May he lead our family with wisdom and power through the good choices he makes.

If any of you lacks wisdom, he should ask God,
who gives generously to all without finding fault,
and it will be given to him.
James 1:5

FATHERHOOD

Father God, thank you that _(your husband's name)_ is such an amazing father to our children. Please continue to instill in him the desire to never exasperate our children, but instead to bring them up in the training and instruction of the Lord. As our heavenly Father and perfect Fatherly example, give him insight and understanding in how to be a good, loving and gracious Father.

Fathers, do not exasperate your children; instead, bring them up in the training and instruction of the Lord.
Ephesians 6:4

_____

_____

_____

_____

_____

FRIENDSHIPS

Father, I pray that you would provide (*your husband's name*) with solid, godly friends he can confide in and trust. Bless these relationships so that they may sharpen one another and influence one another to become more like you. Please protect him from any "friends" who may be causing him to stumble. Give my husband discernment in choosing those with whom he invests most of his time.

As iron sharpens iron, so one man sharpens another.
Proverbs 27:17

_____

_____

_____

_____

_____

PRIORITIES

Father, thank you for providing us with a perfect prescription for our priorities. I pray that (*your husband's name*) would seek first your kingdom and your righteousness. May he consistently look to you and your Word for direction and guidance. Please put his priorities in perfect order and fill him with grace and wisdom to maintain them.

But seek first his kingdom and his righteousness, and all these things will be given to you as well.
Matthew 6:33

_____

_____

_____

_____

_____

REPUTATION

Lord, I pray that as (*your husband's name*)'s wife, I am careful to promote a positive reputation for him. Please guard my lips from saying anything that would show him disrespect or make people think poorly of him. Protect my husband's name from anyone or anything that threatens to tarnish it.

A good name is more desirable than great riches;
to be esteemed is better than silver or gold.
Proverbs 22:1

_____

_____

_____

_____

_____

TRIALS

Lord, as (*your husband's name*) goes through trials, I pray that he would consider it pure joy because he knows that the testing of his faith develops perseverance. Perseverance must finish its work so that he may be mature and complete, not lacking anything. Give my husband an eternal perspective through his hard times so that he does not miss your hand in the process. Thank you for loving my husband enough to fine-tune him so that he becomes more like you.

Consider it pure joy, my brothers, whenever you face trials of any kind, because you know that the testing of your faith develops perseverance. Perseverance must finish its work so that you may be mature and complete, not lacking anything.
James 1:2-3

_____

_____

_____

_____

_____

FEARS

Heavenly Father, I thank you that when (*your husband's name*) seeks you, you answer him and deliver him from all his fears. I know that he, as a man, has some very different fears and concerns than I do, so I pray that you would reach out to him in a very specific way today. Bring to light those things in his mind that he genuinely fears so that he can place them in your protective care.

> *I sought the Lord, and he answered me;*
> *he delivered me from all my fears.*
> *Psalm 34:4*

———————————————————————

———————————————————————

———————————————————————

———————————————————————

———————————————————————

PROTECTION

God, I pray that you would protect and rescue (*your husband's name*) because he loves you and acknowledges your name. When he calls upon you, thank you for answering him and promising to be with him in trouble, delivering him and honoring him along the way. Bless my husband with a long, rich and satisfying life, I pray.

"Because he loves me," says the Lord, "I will rescue him;
I will protect him, for he acknowledges my name.
He will call upon me, and I will answer him;
I will be with him in trouble, I will deliver him and honor him.
With long life will I satisfy him
and show him my salvation."
Psalm 91:14-16

_____

_____

_____

_____

_____

HEALTH

Father God, thank you for being our Healer. Just as you promised to restore and heal the land of Jerusalem, I pray that you would heal *(your husband's name)* of any aliment or disease. Restore his body and keep it working in perfect order. Bless my husband with good health and allow him to enjoy an abundance of peace and security that is found only in you.

> *...I will heal my people and*
> *will let them enjoy abundant peace and security.*
> *Jeremiah 33:6*

_____

_____

_____

_____

_____

PAST

Lord, I pray that if there is something from the past that is causing pain or hardship for (*your husband's name*) that you would tend to him today. By your strength, enable him to forget about the former things and not dwell any longer on the past. I pray on his behalf that you would do a new thing in his life today. Where there once was a desert, a wasteland, or a lonely pit, fill him instead with your living water. Spring up in him now as I pray and wash away the pain of his past. Thank you in advance that through you the old has gone and the new has come.

Forget the former things; do not dwell on the past.
See, I am doing a new thing! Now it springs up; do you not
perceive it? I am making a way in the desert
and streams in the wasteland.
Isaiah 43:18-1

_____

_____

_____

_____

_____

FINANCES

Father God, I pray that you would give (*your husband's name*) wisdom when dealing with the money you provide for him. Teach him to be a good steward of your resources and give him a cheerful heart when giving back to you. I thank you that you promise to supply all of our needs according to your riches in glory. Teach us both how to trust in your hand for provision, not our own.

My God shall supply all your needs according to His riches in glory by Christ Jesus.
Philippians 4:19

_____

_____

_____

_____

_____

CONTENTMENT

Father God, teach (*your husband's name*) how to be content in any and every situation, whether fed or hungry, whether living in plenty or in want. In a world that is consumed with wanting more and with keeping up with those around us, please give my husband a different perspective that is focused solely on you and your Word. May he hold fast to the secret of drawing his strength from your power and your promises to provide for his every need.

...I have learned the secret of being content in any and every situation, whether fed or hungry, whether living in plenty or in want. I can do everything through him who gives me strength.
Philippians 4:12-13

_____

_____

_____

_____

_____

OBEDIENCE

Father God, grow (*your husband's name*) into a man who follows you with wholehearted obedience. Oh that his ways would be steadfast in obeying your decrees! Draw him to your Word so that he can hear from you and do what you say. In every area of his live, give him the desire to submit to your authority and obey your commands. Where he is struggling in obedience, strengthen him. Where he is resisting obedience, convict him. Teach my husband how to follow your commands, I pray. You are our Master and King. We submit to your leadership and rule.

Oh, that my ways were steadfast
in obeying your decrees!
Psalm 119:5

_____

_____

_____

_____

_____

SELF-CONTROL

Father, give (*your husband's name*) strength to exhibit self-control in thought, word and deed, finding comfort and protection within the boundaries you have given him. Put a bad taste in his mouth for those daily indulgences and worldly pleasures that can so easily lead him astray. By your power, strengthen my husband with the discipline of self-control so that he can live an upright, godly life.

Like a city whose walls are broken down
is a man who lacks self-control.
Proverbs 25:28

_____

_____

_____

_____

_____

REPENTANCE

Father God, I pray that you would bring to light any sin in (*your husband's name*)'s life that he has not dealt with. Give him the humility and strength to respond to your call of repentance. I pray that he doesn't just feel bad about the sin in his life, but that he chooses to turn his back to it and walk away. Thank you for promising to forgive and restore those who genuinely seek after you.

I have not come to call the righteous,
but sinners to repentance.
Luke 5:32

_____

_____

_____

_____

_____

GUILT

Lord, please remove any guilt that is hanging over (*your husband's name*)'s life today. Enable him to draw near to you with a sincere heart in full assurance of faith, having his heart sprinkled to cleanse him from a guilty conscience. I thank you that you are a God that convicts so that we know when we stray. Give him wisdom to not buy into the guilt that Satan tries to throw his way in hopes of masking your never-ending forgiveness for him.

Let us draw near to God with a sincere heart in full assurance
of faith, having our hearts sprinkled
to cleanse us from a guilty conscience and
having our bodies washed with pure water.
Hebrews 10:22

_____

_____

_____

_____

_____

WALK

Jesus, I pray that you would authenticate (_your husband's name_)'s relationship with you in a new way today. We know that the kingdom of God is not a matter of talk but of power, so I pray that you would reveal your power in his life like never before. Show yourself as an active and living presence in his everyday life and allow his walk to always match his talk.

For the kingdom of God is not a matter of talk but of power.
1 Corinthians 4:20

_____

_____

_____

_____

_____

UNDIVIDED HEART

Lord, thank you for giving (_your husband's name_) a heart to know you—that you are God. Teach him your way, O Lord, that he may walk in your truth. Give him an undivided heart, that he may fear your name. There are so many things in this world vying for his attention. Please give my husband the desire and discipline to focus solely on you.

Teach me your way, O Lord, and I will walk in your truth;
give me an undivided heart, that I may fear your name.
Psalm 86:11

_____

_____

_____

_____

_____

PRAYER LIFE

Lord, I pray that (_your husband's name_) is a man of prayer. Give him faith to trust in you at all times and pour out his heart to you on a regular basis. Thank you for being a worthy and safe place for my husband to unload his burdens. Give him the desire to seek after you through an intimate prayer life, I pray.

Trust in him at all times, O people;
pour out your hearts to him, for God is our refuge.
Psalm 62:8

_____

_____

_____

_____

_____

FAITH

Jesus, I pray that (*your husband's name*) is a man of faith. May he not go through life as the Babylonians did, trusting in themselves and their own strength, instead of trusting in you. Give him the faith to trust in the unseen and to depend on you for his every step. Humble him, if you must, so that he will rely on you because apart from you, he can do nothing.

"See, he is puffed up; his desires are not upright—but the righteous will live by his faith"
Habakkuk 2:4

_____

_____

_____

_____

_____

DIRECTION

Father God, I pray that you direct (*your husband's name*)'s footsteps according to your Word. Let your light and truth guide him. I pray that he makes time to rest in your presence so that he may become familiar with your ways and attentive to your voice. Guide my husband ever towards you, I pray. Thank you for promising to always go before us and guide us every step of the way.

Send forth your light and your truth, let them guide me;
let them bring me to your holy mountain,
to the place where you dwell.
Psalm 43:3

LAZINESS

Lord, I pray against any laziness in (_your husband's name_). Whether at home or in the office, I pray that you would give him the energy he needs to get his job done well. Please bless all of his efforts and reward him for all of his hard work. Where he is lacking in vision, drive or ambition, be all the inspiration he needs to finish his race strong.

> _If a man is lazy, the rafters sag;_
> _if his hands are idle, the house leaks._
> _Ecclesiastes 10:18_

_____

_____

_____

_____

_____

WORRIES

Father God, I pray against worry in (_your husband's name_) life because I know that worry is a sign of misplaced trust. Your word commands us not to worry about tomorrow, for tomorrow will worry about itself. Please give my husband wisdom to plan and prepare for tomorrow, and faith to leave the details up to you. Thank you for being the God who sees his needs before they arise and makes provision for them.

Therefore do not worry about tomorrow, for tomorrow will worry about itself. Each day has enough trouble of its own.
Matthew 6:34

RECEIVING COMPASSION

Lord, I pray that (*your husband's name*) experiences your compassion and mercy in a rich way today. Because of your great love for him, my husband will not be consumed, for your compassions never fail. They are new every morning; great is your faithfulness. What a promise: to get a do-over; to start with a clean slate and a full supply of all that we need to get through the day. I pray that my husband receives the bounty of this promise in you today.

Because of the Lord's great love we are not consumed,
for his compassions never fail.
They are new every morning; great is your faithfulness.
Lamentations 3:22-23

_____

_____

_____

_____

_____

PROVISION

Father God, in your Word you promise to meet all of our needs according to your glorious riches in Christ Jesus. Thank you for fulfilling this promise in (*your husband's name*) life. I pray that you would open his eyes so that he can see all the many ways that you have richly provided for him. Give him a proper perspective about the difference between his wants and needs so that he can rightfully praise you for all you have done.

And my God will meet all your needs
according to his glorious riches in Christ Jesus.
Philippians 4:19

SOLITUDE

Lord, I pray that you would instill in _(your husband's name)_ the importance of being still before you in solitude. Give him the desire to walk away from his day-to-day distractions for a time so that he can rest with you. Thank you in advance for meeting him in this place so that he can experience more of the fullness found only in you.

> _Be still and know that I am God;_
> _I will be exalted among the nations,_
> _I will be exalted in the earth._
> _Psalm 46:10_

———————————————————

———————————————————

———————————————————

———————————————————

———————————————————

INTEGRITY

Jesus, please grow (<u>*your husband's name*</u>) into a man of integrity. Enable him to stand up for what is right without wavering. I pray that through his integrity you will uphold him and allow him to remain in your presence forever. Thank you for being our God, full of grace and truth. Please strengthen him in integrity so that he more closely resembles the very nature of you.

In my integrity you uphold me and
set me in your presence forever.
Psalm 41:12

_____

_____

_____

_____

_____

HYPOCRISY

Father, I pray against any form of hypocrisy that may be found in (*your husband's name*). I pray that his relationship with you is more than just a form of lip service. Please ignite the flame in his heart so that he will burn with a genuine passion for you. Challenge him to continually maintain a walk that reflects his talk so that others are drawn to the true nature of you.

The Lord says, "These people come near to me with their mouth and honor me with their lips, but their hearts are far from me. Their worship of me is made up only of rules taught by men."
Isaiah 29:13

_____

_____

_____

_____

_____

FAVOR

Jesus, I thank you that through your death on the cross, (*your husband's name*) can stand before you as the righteousness of God. May your unmerited favor rest upon him today, I pray. I hold fast to the promise that you will bless him and surround him with your favor as a shield. Please enable me to never take for granted the power of your favor and the way it protects him each and every day.

For surely, O LORD, you bless the righteous;
you surround them with your favor as with a shield.
Psalm 5:12

_____

_____

_____

_____

_____

COURAGE

Father God, I pray that you would grow (*your husband's name*) into a man of great courage. When facing trials, embolden him with the power of your presence so that he can stand firm. In the face of opposition and fear, be brave through him, I pray. Thank you for the promise that you are always with him. In moments of trouble, remind him that you are with him, protecting, delivering, upholding and sustaining him all of his days.

Have I not commanded you? Be strong and courageous. Do not be terrified; do not be discouraged, for the LORD your God will be with you wherever you go.
Joshua 1:9

_____

_____

_____

_____

_____

HUMILITY

Lord, I pray against any pride that threatens to rear its ugly head in (*your husband's name*) life. Instead, may he clothe himself with humility towards you and towards man. Teach him how to live as you did—fully giving up your rights in order to obey the Father and serve man. Thank you for the promise of grace poured out in abundance on those who choose the way of humility.

All of you, clothe yourselves with humility toward one another,
because, God opposes the proud
but gives grace to the humble.
1 Peter 5:6

_____

_____

_____

_____

_____

SERVANTS HEART

Father God, I pray that in everything (*your husband's name*) does that he serve wholeheartedly, as if he were serving you, not men. In a world that is obsessed with looking out for number one, give my husband a heart that is willing to put others before himself in order to serve them well. Thank you for your perfect example of showing strength through service.

Serve wholeheartedly,
as if you were serving the Lord, not men.
Ephesians 6:7

_____

_____

_____

_____

_____

FREEDOM

God, thank you for the freedom we have in Jesus. By your power, enable (*your husband's name*) to stand firm in the freedom you have so graciously provided him. When he is burdened by the weight of chains that once enslaved him, whisper words of truth into his heart. You have set him free! May he live in the light and power of this truth all the days of his life.

It is for freedom that Christ has set us free. Stand firm, then,
and do not let yourselves be burdened again
by a yoke of slavery.
Galatians 5:1

_____

_____

_____

_____

_____

WORDS

Jesus, set a guard over (*your husband's name*) mouth, and keep watch over the door of his lips. May the words he speaks today be helpful for building up those around him according to their specific needs. Impress upon my husband the power of the words he speaks—words that have the potential to bring life or death to those around him. Block any words that come from his mouth if they are not intended to benefit the one receiving them.

Set a guard over my mouth, O LORD;
keep watch over the door of my lips.
Psalm 141:3

_____

_____

_____

_____

_____

PEACE

Father God, thank you for the incredible gift of peace that is ours in Jesus. I thank you that we don't have to live as the world lives, getting caught up and distracted by every circumstance that comes our way. Instead, fix (*your husband's name*) mind steadfast on you so that he can rest in your perfect peace. Let it be your peace that guides him in all his decision making, and guard his heart and mind with your protective peace, I pray.

> *The Lord gives his people strength.*
> *The Lord blesses them with peace.*
> *Psalm 29:11*

_____

_____

_____

_____

_____

UNBELIEF

Father, we know that without faith it is impossible to please you, so please pour out faith in abundance on (*your husband's name*). Where he is struggling with unbelief, reach out your hand and show yourself faithful so that he will place his full weight on you. Lord, my husband believes. Help him overcome his unbelief!

> *I do believe; help me overcome my unbelief!*
> *Mark 9:24*

_____

_____

_____

_____

_____

AS A HUSBAND

Father God, as I bow before you, I lay all selfish agenda aside and ask that you strengthen (*your husband's name*) in his role as my husband. I can't begin to grasp this command that you have given him—to love me as Christ has loved the church, giving himself up for her. By your Spirit, teach him what it means to love me well. And as he abides in you, love me through my husband, I pray.

Husbands, love your wives, just as Christ loved the church and gave himself up for her.
Ephesians 5:25

DESIRE FOR THE WORD

Father God, open (*your husband's name*) eyes that he may see the wonderful things in your law. Give him an unquenchable desire for your Word so that he can live according to your truth. Thank you for the rich satisfaction of your presence found in your Truth. Reveal yourself to my husband through your Word in a fresh way today, I pray.

Open my eyes that I may see
the wonderful things in your law.
Psalm 119:18

_____

_____

_____

_____

_____

FOR YOUR LITTLES

SALVATION

Father, today I pray that you would show (*your child's name*) your amazing and unfailing love in a unique and personal way. Please open up his (her) heart and grant him (her) your salvation at an early age. May my child have a genuine hunger and thirst for you every day of his (her) life.

Show us your unfailing love, O Lord,
and grant us your salvation.
Psalm 85:7

_____

_____

_____

_____

_____

LOVE AND ACCEPTANCE

Father God, I pray that (*your child's name*) feels loved and accepted. Give him (her) understanding to grasp how complete your love is for him (her). May my child be so grounded in your love and acceptance for him (her) that he (she) never falls into doubt. Thank you for loving my child before he (she) could ever love you and for choosing him (her) to be holy and blameless in your sight.

For he chose us in him before the creation of the world to be holy and blameless in his sight. In love he predestined us to be adopted as his sons through Jesus Christ, in accordance with his pleasure and will—to the praise of his glorious grace, which he has freely given us in the One he loves.
Ephesians 1:2-6

_____

_____

_____

_____

_____

IDENTITY

God, I pray that you would create in (*your child's name*) a healthy self-esteem that is rooted in his (her) identity in you. Help him (her) to understand that he (she) is your masterpiece, created by a perfect God who does not make mistakes. Please instill the same truth in me so that I can be a good example to him (her).

For we are God's workmanship, created in Christ Jesus to do good works, which God prepared in advance for us to do.
Ephesians 2:10

_____

_____

_____

_____

_____

TRUST

Father God, reveal yourself to (*your child's name*) so that he (she) will put his (her) trust in you. Day by day, teach him (her) to trust in you with all his (her) heart, leaning on your ways and your truth to guide him (her). This world and the people in it are sure to let my child down, but you will never fail him (her). Thank you for being a rock that he (she) can stand on, a faithful companion for all his (her) days.

Trust in the Lord with all your heart
and lean not on your own understanding;
in all your ways acknowledge him,
and he will make your paths straight.
Proverbs 3:5-6

_____

_____

_____

_____

_____

SELF-CONTROL

Father God, I pray that you would teach (*your child's name*) at an early age what it means to live a life of self-control. I pray that he (she) say "no" to ungodliness and worldly passions and that he (she) live a self-controlled, upright and godly life. May my child find comfort and protection within the boundaries you have given him (her) through your Word, I pray.

For the grace of God that brings salvation has appeared to all men. It teaches us to say "No" to ungodliness and worldly passions, and to live self-controlled, upright and godly lives in this present age.
Titus 2:11-12

_____

_____

_____

_____

_____

LIVING BY AND LOVING GOD'S WORD

Father, I pray that (*your child's name*) would learn to live according to your word. I pray that he (she) would seek you with all of his (her) heart so that he (she) does not stray from your commands. Hide your word in his (her) heart that he (she) may not sin against you. Please give my child a love for your Word at an early age so that he (she) desires to know and obey all you ask of him (her).

How can a young man keep his way pure?
By living according to your word. I seek you with all my heart;
do not let me stray from your commands.
I have hidden your word in my heart that
I might not sin against you.
Psalm 119:9-11

_____

_____

_____

_____

_____

FEAR

Father God, I pray against any fear that threatens to overcome (*your child's name*) now or in the future. I pray that he (she) would understand that you are a sovereign and powerful God that is greater than any threat that can come before him (her). I pray that my child would not fear, because you are with him (her). Please strengthen him (her), help him (her), and uphold him (her) with your righteous right hand.

So do not fear, for I am with you; do not be dismayed, for I am
your God. I will strengthen you and help you;
I will uphold you with my righteous right hand.
Isaiah 41:10

_____

_____

_____

_____

_____

UNIQUE IDENTITY

Father, I pray that (*your child's name*) would live his (her) life as the person that you have created him (her) to be. Thank you for calling him (her) "a chosen people, a royal priesthood, a holy nation, a people belonging to God, that *he (she)* may declare the praises of him who called *him (her)* out of darkness into his wonderful light". Give me eyes to see my child as you do so that I don't miss out on the creative wonder that he (she) is in you.

*But you are a chosen people, a royal priesthood, a holy nation, a
people belonging to God, that you may declare the praises of
him who called you out of darkness
into his wonderful light.
1 Peter 2:9*

HONESTY

Lord, I pray that (*your child's name*) would walk blamelessly, choose what is righteous and speak the truth from his (her) heart. Please fulfill your promise that "he who does these things will never be shaken". I pray that every time a dishonest word leaves my child's mouth, you would instantly convict him (her) of it. I pray that his (her) life would be marked by integrity and truth.

He whose walk is blameless and who does what is righteous,
who speaks the truth from his heart…..
He who does these things will never be shaken.
Psalm 15:2,5

_____

_____

_____

_____

_____

RESISTING REBELLION

Lord, I pray that (*your child's name*) would be willing to be obedient to you so that he (she) may benefit from your blessings. Please give him (her) strength to resist rebellion, which opens the door to trouble and heartache. Thank you that even now you can begin to prepare my child's heart and soften him (her) so that he (she) desires to choose you all the days of his (her) life.

If you are willing and obedient, you will eat the best from the land; but if you resist and rebel, you will be devoured by the sword. For the mouth of the Lord has spoken.
Isaiah 1:19

_____

_____

_____

_____

_____

GRATITUDE

Jesus, I pray that (*your child's name*) would learn to give thanks in all circumstances, for this is your will for him (her) in Christ Jesus. Whether singing songs of praise from a mountaintop or crying out to you in a valley, I pray that he (she) would have the attitude of gratitude in every circumstance of his (her) life. Thank you for being more than worthy of our praise.

Give thanks in all circumstances,
for this is God's will for you in Christ Jesus.
1 Thessalonians 5:18

_____

_____

_____

_____

_____

WALKING IN TRUTH

Father God, give (*your child's name*) the desire to know your truth. Guide him (her) in your truth and teach him (her). Thank you for giving us your Word of Truth. I pray that my child is attracted to truth and repulsed by lies so that he (she) can walk in the freedom that you so graciously provide.

Guide me in your truth and teach me, for you are God my
Savior, and my hope is in you all day long.
Psalm 25:5

_____

_____

_____

_____

_____

LOVING OTHERS

Lord, make your love increase and overflow from (*your child's name*) to those around him (her). I pray that you give him (her) an understanding of your measureless love and open his (her) heart to experience the security and joy found in a relationship with you. Set my child apart because of the way he (she) genuinely loves others, I pray.

May the Lord make your love increase and overflow for each
other and for everyone else, just as ours does for you.
1 Thessalonians 3:12

_____

_____

_____

_____

_____

COURAGE

Father, I pray that (*your child's name*) be strong and courageous in character and in actions. Give him (her) confidence in the fact that you are always with him (her) and will never leave or forsake him (her). Thank you that when my child is weak, you are strong, for your power is made perfect in his (her) weakness.

Be strong and courageous.
Do not be afraid or terrified because of them,
for the Lord your God goes with you;
he will never leave you nor forsake you.
Deuteronomy 31:6

_____

_____

_____

_____

_____

PROTECTION

God, please protect (_your child's name_) from any harm or trouble that may come his (her) way. Command your angels concerning my child to guard him (her) in all his (her) ways. I release this precious one into your care today, knowing that you are his (her) only true protector. Forgive me for the fear I have in relinquishing that control over to you. Thank you for loving my child more than I do and for being with him (her) always, especially when I'm not.

For he will command his angels concerning you
to guard you in all your ways."
Psalm 91:11

_____

_____

_____

_____

_____

PURITY

Father, I pray for (*your child's name*) to live a life of purity in thought, word and deed. Teach him (her) at an early age to live according to your word, to seek you with all of his (her) heart and to walk according to your commands. Thank you that as he (she) begins to etch your word on his (her) heart, you give him (her) the desire and the strength to remain pure. Protect my child's heart from deception and give him (her) a desire to be wholly devoted to you.

How can a young man keep his way pure? By living according to your word. I seek you with all my heart; do not let me stray from your commands. I have hidden your word in my heart that I might not sin against you.
Psalm 119:9-11

_____

_____

_____

_____

_____

JOY

Father, I pray that (*your child's name*) live a life filled with joy. May the joy of the Lord be his (her) strength! No matter what life brings his (her) way, teach him (her) to hold fast to his (her) faith and hope in you, and fill him (her) with your joy. I pray that people would be drawn to my child and come to know you because of the joy they see in him (her).

> *...the joy of the Lord is your strength.*
> *Nehemiah 8:10*

_____

_____

_____

_____

_____

GODLY FRIENDS

Lord, I pray that in every stage of (_your child's name_)'s life that you would provide him (her) with solid, godly friends. Teach my child to be cautious with his (her) friendships and draw him (her) only to those who resemble you. Give him (her) wisdom and discernment when developing these relationships and cast away all those who may lead my child astray. Bless him (her) with friends that will challenge and sharpen him (her) all the days of his (her) life.

A righteous man is cautious in friendship,
but the way of the wicked leads them astray.
Proverbs 12:26

_____

_____

_____

_____

_____

FORGIVENESS

Lord, grant that (*your child's name*) be kind and compassionate in his (her) relationships, forgiving others just as in Christ you forgave him (her). Teach him (her) how to keep short accounts and how to extend forgiveness with ease. I pray that my child never allow pride to hold him (her) back from showing forgiveness to those around him (her).

Be kind and compassionate to one another, forgiving each other,
just as in Christ God forgave you.
Ephesians 4:32

_____

_____

_____

_____

_____

SERVANT'S HEART

Father God, I pray that in everything that (*your child's name*) does that he (she) serve wholeheartedly, as if he (she) were serving you, not men. In a world that is obsessed with looking out for number one, give my child a heart that is willing to put others before himself (herself). Thank you for your perfect example of showing strength through service. Please teach my child to follow wholeheartedly after you.

Serve wholeheartedly,
as if you were serving the Lord, not men.
Ephesians 6:7

_____

_____

_____

_____

_____

PERSEVERANCE

Father God, since (<u>*your child's name*</u>) is surrounded by such a great cloud of witnesses, show him (her) how to throw off everything that hinders and the sin that so easily entangles. Let him (her) run with perseverance the race marked out for him (her). I pray that my child doesn't always look for the easy way out, but exhibits patient endurance through hardships. Develop in him (her) this supernatural kind of perseverance so that he (she) may be mature and complete, not lacking in anything.

Therefore, since we are surrounded by such a great cloud of witnesses, let us throw off everything that hinders and the sin that so easily entangles, and let us run with perseverance the race marked out for us.
Hebrews 12:1

_____

_____

_____

_____

_____

HOPE

Lord, may you, the God of hope, fill (*your child's name*) with all joy and peace as he (she) trusts in you, so that he (she) may overflow with hope by the power of the Holy Spirit. Thank you for the hope in your promises, the hope of a future, and the hope of a life in eternity with you. May my child always walk in the hope of your amazing glory.

May the God of hope fill you with all joy and peace
as you trust in him, so that you may overflow
with hope by the power of the Holy Spirit.
Romans 15:13

_____

_____

_____

_____

_____

PRAYER

Father God, I pray that you impress upon (*your child's name*) the importance of prayer at an early age. Teach him (her) to be joyful always; pray continuously; give thanks in all circumstances, for this is God's will for him (her) in Christ Jesus. May my child's first inclination in all circumstances be to go to you first in prayer. I thank you in advance for always hearing his (her) prayers and answering them according to your good, pleasing and perfect will.

Be joyful always; pray continuously; give thanks in all circumstances, for this is God's will for you in Christ Jesus.
1 Thessalonians 5:16-18

_____

_____

_____

_____

_____

BEING A LIGHT

God, I pray that you would make (*your child's name*) a light in this world full of darkness. Let his (her) light shine before men, that they may see his (her) good deeds and praise you in heaven. I thank you in advance for transforming my child's life so that he (she) may reflect your light and your amazing glory.

In the same way, let your light shine before men, that they may see your good deeds and praise your Father in heaven.
Matthew 5:16

_____

_____

_____

_____

_____

HEALTH

Lord, I pray that you would bless (*your child's name*) with a life of good health. If any ailment or disease should come into his (her) body, restore him (her) to health and heal all his (her) wounds. Thank you that you have power to overcome any disease or death. Give me boldness to call upon you when my child is ill and faith to trust in your power to miraculously heal him (her) in every way.

But I will restore you to health and heal your wounds.
Jeremiah 30:17

_____

_____

_____

_____

_____

WISDOM

Lord, I pray that (*your child's name*) live a life seasoned with wisdom. If he (she) lacks wisdom, remind him (her) to ask you, who gives generously to all without finding fault. I also pray that my child's choices always reflect you and your Word, and that he (she) leads others by example into your infinite wisdom and truth.

If any of you lacks wisdom, he should ask God, who givens generously to all without finding fault, and it will be given to him. James 1:5

_____

_____

_____

_____

_____

ROLE MODELS

Lord, I pray that as (*your child's name*) goes through each stage of his (her) life that you would provide godly role models for him (her). I know that there will come a time when my husband and I will no longer be my child's main source of influence, so I pray that you would provide him (her) with other adults who will speak truth into his (her) life. May he (she) only be drawn to those who advise according to your Word so that he (she) walks with the wise. Bless these relationships in his (her) life, I pray.

He who walks with the wise grows wise,
but a companion of fools suffers harm.
Proverbs 13:20

_____

_____

_____

_____

_____

FAITH

Jesus, I pray that you would grow (*your child's name*) into a man (woman) of great faith. Give him (her) understanding that without faith it is impossible to please you, because anyone who comes to you must believe that you exist and that you reward those who earnestly seek you. I pray that my child gets to know and appreciate you as the Great I Am and can grasp that you are ever present in every single second of his (her) life.

And without faith it is impossible to please God, because anyone who comes to him must believe that he exists and that he rewards those who earnestly seek him.
Hebrews 11:6

_____

_____

_____

_____

_____

FREEDOM

Father God, thank you for the gift of your Word. I pray that at an early age you would lead (*your child's name*) to the truth found in your word. Penetrate your words of truth in his (her) heart and teach him (her) to apply these truths to every area of his (her) life so that he (she) can experience the freedom you so graciously provide.

Then you will know the truth, and the truth will set you free.
John 8:32

_____

_____

_____

_____

_____

OBEDIENCE

Lord, I pray that (*your child's name*) would be willing and obedient so that he (she) may experience the very best from you. Thank you that even now you can begin to prepare my child's heart and soften him (her) to make good choices. From the small things when he (she) is little to the bigger things as he (she) grows, please give my child strength to resist all forms of rebellion so that he (she) can experience your very best.

If you are willing and obedient, you will eat the best from the land; but if you resist and rebel, you will be devoured by the sword. For the mouth of the Lord has spoken.
Isaiah 1:19

_____

_____

_____

_____

_____

COMPLAINING

Heavenly Father, I pray that (*your child's name*) does everything without complaining or arguing, so that he (she) may become blameless and pure. As a child of God, may he (she) be found without fault in this crooked and depraved generation. Set him (her) apart from the pollution of this world by cleansing his (her) thoughts and attitudes so that he (she) can shine for you.

Do everything without complaining or arguing, so that you may become blameless and pure, children of God without fault in a crooked and depraved generation
Philippians 2:14-15

_____

_____

_____

_____

_____

CONVICTIONS

Heavenly Father, make (*your child's name*) strong and courageous, careful to obey your word with unwavering truth. Give him (her) the conviction to stand up for what is right, even when it seems like he (she) is the only one standing. Thank you for your promise to always be with him (her) and strengthen him (her) all the days of his (her) life.

Be strong and courageous. Be careful to obey all the law my servant Moses gave you; do not turn from it to the right or to the left, that you may be successful wherever you go.
Joshua 1:7

_____

_____

_____

_____

_____

RESPECT AUTHORITY

Father God, instill in my child the importance of respecting authority. We know that all authority is given by you so we humbly submit to our leaders, whatever their level. Teach (*your child's name*) that whether or not he (she) agrees with or even likes the leaders you have placed over him (her), he (she) must respect them in their position as they submit to you.

Everyone must submit himself to the governing authorities, for there is no authority except that which God has established.
Romans 13:1

_____

_____

_____

_____

_____

WORRY

Heavenly Father, I pray that (*your child's name*) learn at an early age that he (she) can cast his (her) cares on you because you love him (her) so very much. Thank you for being more than able to carry each care—each burden—each worry for my child so that he (she) doesn't have to. Pour out faith on my child in abundance so that he (she) will trust in you.

Cast all your anxiety on him
because he cares for you.
1 Peter 5:7

_____

_____

_____

_____

_____

STRENGTH

Father God, thank you for being our refuge and our strength—our ever-present help in times of trouble. Please grow (*your child's name*) into a man (woman) of great strength. Train him (her) to depend on you when he (she) is weary, trusting in you to be all the strength he (she) needs. I thank you that when my child is weak, you are strong, for your power is made perfect in his (her) weakness.

I can do everything through him
who gives me strength.
Philippians 4:13

_____

_____

_____

_____

_____

MIND

Lord, protect (*your child's name*) mind from the lies of the enemy. Teach him (her) how to take each thought captive to make it obedient to you. Please give him (her) the desire to fill his (her) mind with your Word so that he (she) can distinguish the truth from lies. Thank you that when my child turns his (her) thoughts towards you, you promise to guard his (her) heart and mind with a peace beyond all understanding.

We demolish arguments and every pretension that sets itself up against the knowledge of God, and we take captive every thought to make it obedient to Christ.
2 Corinthians 10:5

_____

_____

_____

_____

_____

PEACE

Father God, thank you for the incredible gift of peace that is ours in Jesus. I thank you that we don't have to live as the world lives, getting caught up and distracted by every circumstance that comes our way. Instead, fix (*your child's name*) mind steadfast on you so that he (she) can rest in your perfect peace. Let it be your peace that guides my child in all his (her) ways, and guard his (her) heart and mind with your protective peace, I pray.

You will keep in perfect peace him whose mind is steadfast,
because he trusts in you.
Isaiah 26:3

_____

_____

_____

_____

_____

FAVOR

Jesus, I pray that (*your child's name*) would grow in wisdom and stature, and in favor with God and man. May your unmerited favor rest upon him (her) as he (she) trusts in you. I hold fast to the promise that you will bless my child and surround him (her) with your favor as a shield. Please enable me to never take for granted the power of your favor and the way it protects my child all the days of his (her) life.

> *And Jesus grew in wisdom and stature,*
> *and in favor with God and men.*
> *Luke 2:52*

_____

_____

_____

_____

_____

TEMPTATIONS

Father, I pray against any temptations that may come before (_your child's name_). I pray that he (she) would literally hate what is evil and cling to what is good. Thank you for the truth that you reveal to us through your Word. Please guard my child's mind from being lured by Satan's lies and draw him (her) toward truth. Give him (her) the strength and courage to flee from temptations, to deny the desires of his (her) flesh and to walk in the power of the Spirit all the days of his (her) life.

Hate what is evil; cling to what is good.
Romans 12:9

_____

_____

_____

_____

_____

HONORING PARENTS

Father God, thank you for the privilege you have given me to be the parent of (_your child's name_). As I look to you for wisdom and guidance in parenting him (her) well, I pray that you would instill in my child the importance of obeying and respecting me as his (her) parent. I hold fast to the promise that as he (she) honors me, you will bless him (her) with a long and joyful life.

Children, obey your parents in the Lord, for this is right.
"Honor your father and mother"—which is the first
commandment with a promise—"that it will go well with you
and that you may enjoy long life on earth."
Ephesians 6:1-3

_____

_____

_____

_____

_____

WORDS

Jesus, set a guard over (_your child's name_) mouth, and keep watch over the door of his (her) lips. May the words he (she) speaks today be helpful for building up those around him (her) according to their specific needs. Impress upon my child the power of the words he (she) speaks—words that have the potential to bring life or death to those around him (her). Block any words that come from his (her) mouth if they are not intended to benefit the one receiving them.

Set a guard over my mouth, O LORD;
keep watch over the door of my lips.
Psalm 141:3

_____

_____

_____

_____

_____

REPENTANCE

Father God, I pray that you would bring to light any sin in (*your child's name*)'s life that he (she) has not dealt with. Give him (her) the humility and strength to respond to your call of repentance. I pray that my child doesn't just feel bad about the sin in his (her) life, but that he (she) chooses to turn his (her) back to it and walk away. Thank you for promising to forgive and restore those who genuinely seek after you.

I have not come to call the righteous,
but sinners to repentance.
Luke 5:32

FOR YOU

DOING GOOD

Father God, I pray that you would enable me as a wife and a mom to not withhold good from my family when it is in my power to act. I know that you give me many opportunities throughout the day to display your goodness, and many times those opportunities are lost on my selfishness or my agenda. Please show me specific ways today that I can do a little good to the ones I hold most dear.

Do not withhold good from those who deserve it,
when it is in your power to act.
Proverbs 3:27

_____

_____

_____

_____

_____

UNITY IN MARRIAGE

Father, I pray (*your husband's name*) and I would be unified in our marriage. As we make decisions for our family, fill us with your grace and mercy so that we can operate as one. Please protect us from Satan, who is determined to divide us and destroy our marriage. May we always look to each other's interests before our own and respect each other in all we do.

Jesus knew their thoughts and said to them, "Every kingdom divided against itself will be ruined, and every city or household divided against itself will not stand."
Matthew 12:25

_____

_____

_____

_____

_____

PERSPECTIVE OF CHILD

Father God, thank you for the child you have blessed me with. Forgive me for buying into the lie some days that my child is a burden or a distraction. Even if those words never come out of my mouth, forgive me for treating him (her) in that way. I believe in the truth of your Word which reminds me that he (she) is a heritage, a reward and a true gift from you. Please teach me how to parent my child in that way every moment of every day.

Sons are a heritage from the Lord,
children a reward from him.
Psalm 127:3

_____

_____

_____

_____

_____

WORRY

Father, enable me today to obey your command that says, "Do not worry". Even though worrying seems like a maternal duty, please release me from the hold that the sin of worry has over my life. I profess to you today that I believe you are more than capable of carrying my today, my tomorrow, and all the moments in between that I somehow manage to worry about.

Therefore do not worry about tomorrow, for tomorrow will worry about itself. Each day has enough trouble of its own.
Matthew 6:34

_____

_____

_____

_____

_____

CONTENTMENT

Lord, I pray for (*your husband's name*) and I to be content with what you have given us in life. We live in a world that is obsessed with "stuff". Please keep us out of that never-ending cycle of discontent and addiction for more. Thank you for your promise to always be by our side to sustain us. I pray that each day we will gain a better understanding of the gravity of that promise. Please continue to focus our affections, our desires and our hunger on you and only you

Keep your lives free from the love of money and be content with what you have, because God has said, "Never will I leave you; never will I forsake you." Hebrews 13:5

_____

_____

_____

_____

_____

PEACEFUL HOME

Father God, it is very important to me to have a home that is considered peaceful to my husband and my kids. I pray that you would teach me how to seek peace and pursue it with my family. Bring to light any ways that I may be creating chaos in my home or personally disturbing the peace. I commit myself to the role of peacemaker in my home.

...he must seek peace and pursue it.
1 Peter 3:11

_____

_____

_____

_____

_____

APPEARANCE

Father, every time I look into the mirror, please remind me that you don't look at the things man looks at. Man looks at the outward appearance, but you look at the heart. Please give me eyes to see myself as you see me, and give me the discipline it takes to invest in the condition of my heart rather than only on the condition of my complexion, waistline or wardrobe.

The Lord does not look at the things man looks at. Man looks at the outward appearance, but the Lord looks at the heart.
1 Samuel 16:7

_____

_____

_____

_____

_____

FULLNESS

Lord, I come to you today seeking your fullness. Most days, I admit, I feel more depleted than full. However, your Word tells me that you have created me for more. I was made to experience the measure of all the fullness of you. What amazing truth! I claim that promise today, and pray that you would give me the power to grasp a deeper understanding of the satisfying fullness of your love for me.

And I pray that you, being rooted and established in love, may have power, together with all the saints, to grasp how wide and long and high and deep is the love of Christ, and to know this love that surpasses all knowledge—that you may be filled to the measure of all the fullness of God.
Ephesians 3:17-19

_____

_____

_____

_____

_____

PRIORITIES

Father God, I can hear you saying these words to me… "(*Your name, your name*) you are worried and upset about many things, but only one thing is needed." Teach me, amid my crazy schedule and all of my responsibilities, to be like Mary and choose to rest in you. Show me a way to guard my schedule and protect my relationship with you so that my time and energies truly reflect my priorities.

"Martha, Martha," the Lord answered, "you are worried and upset about many things, but only one thing is needed. Mary has chosen what is better and it will not be taken away from her."
Luke 10:41-42

TRAINING IN TRUTH

Father, focus my priorities today so that I can honestly say, "I have no greater joy than to hear that my children are walking in the truth". Teach me how to parent to the heart of my children, consistently speaking Truth and living in a way that demonstrates a life lived by the words I speak. Show me throughout my day how to maintain focus on training my little ones and steering them on toward more of you.

I have no greater joy than to hear
that my children are walking in the truth.
3 John 1:4

_____

_____

_____

_____

_____

ENCOURAGEMENT

Father God, enable me to be an encourager for my family today. Give me a greater understanding of the value of an encouraging word and its significance in our everyday battle against sin. Open my eyes and ears to specific, creative ways that I can cheer on each member of my family in order that they maximize their strengths instead of focus on their weaknesses.

But encourage one another daily, as long as it is
called Today, so that none of you may be hardened
by sin's deceitfulness.
Hebrews 3:13

PERSEVERANCE IN PARENTING

Father, I claim this verse today as a mom. I will not become weary or lose heart in doing good or choosing what is right for my kids, because I know that in the right time, during the right season, I will reap a harvest of blessings. Give me the courage and discipline to press on and always keep my eyes on You.

Let us not become weary in doing good, for at the proper time we will reap a harvest if we do not give up.
Galatians 6:9

_____

_____

_____

_____

_____

WORDS

Jesus, I pray that you would set a guard over my mouth, and keep watch over the door of my lips. May the words I speak today be helpful for building up my family according to their specific needs. Block any words coming out of my mouth if they are not intended to benefit the one receiving them.

Set a guard over my mouth, O LORD;
keep watch over the door of my lips.
Psalm 141:3

_____

_____

_____

_____

_____

RESPECT HUSBAND

Father God, I am truly challenged by this verse because I know that you are asking me to respect my husband in a way that is beyond me. You are asking me to notice him, regard him, honor him, prefer him, venerate and esteem him, defer to him, praise him, love him and admire him exceedingly. I thank you that though that kind of love seems beyond me, I know it's not beyond you. Please love my husband through me so that he can experience supernatural love.

…And the wife must respect her husband.
Ephesians 5:33

_____

_____

_____

_____

_____

SATISFACTION

Father God, I pray that this morning you would satisfy me with your unfailing love that I may sing for joy and be glad all my days. Fill me to the brim, completely soaking me in your grace, mercy and love so that I don't spend my day looking for others means of satisfaction. Give me the desire and discipline to always go to you and only you to find my fulfillment.

Satisfy us in the morning with your unfailing love, that we may sing for joy and be glad all our days.
Psalm 90:14

_____

_____

_____

_____

_____

WISDOM

Father God, when I am lacking wisdom and seeking advice throughout my day, I pray that you would remind me of this verse. Remind me that all I have to do is ask you, who gives generously to all without finding fault. Forgive me for so often looking for the instant answer through friends or family instead of turning to you and waiting for your answer.

*If any of you lacks wisdom, he should ask God, who gives
generously to all without finding fault,
and it will be given to him.*
James 1:5

EXPECTATION

Jesus, I come to you today desiring to release my husband from all of the expectations I hold him to. I confess that I have misplaced so much of my hope on him. Instead, teach me how to find rest in you alone, for my expectation and my hope can only be found in and met by you.

Find rest, O my soul, in God alone;
my hope comes from him.
Psalm 62:5

_____

_____

_____

_____

_____

TEMPTATIONS

Lord, thank you that you will never let me be tempted beyond what I can bear. Please give me eyes to see all of the ways out, or escapes, that you provide so that I don't fall into sin. Give me the strength to trust that your power in me is more than enough to withstand any temptation that the evil one tries to throw my way. Fight the battle for me, through me today.

*No temptation has seized you except what is common to man.
And God is faithful; he will not let you be tempted beyond
what you can bear. But when you are tempted, he will also
provide a way out so that you can stand up under it.*
1 Corinthians 10:13

_____

_____

_____

_____

_____

DIRECTION IN PARENTING

Father, as a mom, I feel like so many of the decisions I make for my kids and my family are based on guess work and just doing what I think is best. However, your word teaches me that you will instruct me and teach me in the way I should go. I thank you for taking such a vested interest in the details of my life so that I don't have to parent blindly. Give me ears to hear your counsel, and I will follow after you.

I will instruct you and teach you in the way you should go; I will counsel you and watch over you.
Psalm 32:8

_____

_____

_____

_____

_____

BURDENS

God, forgive me for asking you to help me to carry burdens that you never asked me to carry in the first place. Please give me strength instead to let go of these burdens, to cast them fully on you, trusting that you will sustain me. I thank you that you have great concern for me and never ask me to carry anything that your grace hasn't already covered.

Cast your cares on the LORD and he will sustain you; he will never let the righteous fall.
Psalm 55:22

_____

_____

_____

_____

_____

WEAKNESS

Father God, I praise you today for my weaknesses, because I know that through them, your power is made perfect. Teach me how to rest each moment of my day in your grace and by your strength. When moments of weakness arise, please bring this verse to my mind so that I can praise you...for when I am weak, then I am strong!

But he said to me, "My grace is sufficient for you, for my power is made perfect in weakness." Therefore I will boast all the more gladly about my weaknesses, so that Christ's power may rest on me. That is why, for Christ's sake, I delight in weaknesses, in insults, in hardships, in persecutions, in difficulties. For when I am weak, then I am strong.
2 Corinthians 12:9-10

_____

_____

_____

_____

_____

BE A LIGHT

Father God, I admit that sometimes it's easier to let my light shine before men (in the world) than shine in my own home. I pray that you would provide opportunities for me to let my light shine before my family, that they might see my good deeds and praise you in heaven. Use me to brighten up each of my family member's day in a special way today.

In the same way, let your light shine before men, that they may see your good deeds and praise your Father in heaven.
Matthew 5:16

PERSONAL PROVISION

Lord Jesus, the enormity of your promise to meet ALL of my needs according to your glorious riches leaves me feeling humbled and grateful. You, the very God who created me with all of my unique needs, desire to meet those needs in a unique and wonderful way. Show me today a glimpse of your personal provision for me and I will receive them as gifts from you.

And my God will meet all your needs according to his glorious riches in Christ Jesus.
Philippians 4:19

_____

_____

_____

_____

_____

FORGIVENESS IN MARRIAGE

Father, I thank you for being the ultimate example of forgiveness for me. I pray that you would instill in (*your husband's name*) & I the ability to easily forgive one another. Please expose any area of my life where I am withholding forgiveness from my husband and forgive him through me today, I pray.

Bear with each other and forgive whatever grievances you may have against one another. Forgive as the Lord forgave you.
Colossians 3:13

_____

_____

_____

_____

_____

PRAYER

Jesus, I pray that you would grow in me a prayerful attitude as I go through my day. While driving in the car, set my mind to lifting up those who are my passengers. As I pick up after my family, discipline me to use that time to cover them in prayer. Change what before may have seemed like mindless, mundane and meaningless time spent doing household responsibilities into precious, purposeful and challenging moments of prayer.

Pray continually…
1 Thessalonians 5:17

_____

_____

_____

_____

_____

OPPORTUNITY

Father God, I truly desire to make the most of *every* opportunity I have with my family, especially while my kids are young. Enable me, by your power, to show my children your love, grace and mercy every chance I get. Enable me to honor and respect my husband in all circumstances. Empower me to seize every opportunity to reach out to those around me in need through your wisdom and power, I pray.

Be very careful, then, how you live—not as unwise but as wise,
making the most of every opportunity,
because the days are evil.
Ephesians 5:15-16

_____

_____

_____

_____

_____

INTENTIONAL LIVING

Father God, I know that before I can love and serve my family well, I need to seek you. Forgive me for the days that I decide I can be a super-wife/mom without you. I am reminded afresh that apart from you, I can do nothing. Please fill me today with the desire to live a more intentional life. Like David, give me the discipline to lay myself before you each morning and wait in expectation for you to speak to my heart.

In the morning, O LORD, you hear my voice; in the morning I lay my requests before you and wait in expectation.
Psalm 5:3

_____

_____

_____

_____

_____

HELPMATE

Jesus, I truly desire to bring (*your husband's name*) good, not harm, all the days of my life. As I go through my day, please bring this verse to my mind and check the condition of my heart. Prick my spirit if my words, actions or attitude are hindering rather than helping him in any way. I pray that the way I love and serve my husband brings glory to you each and every day of our lives.

She brings him good, not harm, all the days of her life.
Proverbs 31:12

_____

_____

_____

_____

_____

PEACE

Lord, I pray that you would teach me how to keep my mind steadfast because I could use some perfect peace. Although you have provided me with many people that I can lean on, you are truly the only safe place for me to put my trust. Give me the discipline to seek you first so that no matter what chaos might be going on around me, I can be in perfect peace.

You will keep in perfect peace him whose mind is steadfast,
because he trusts in you.
Isaiah 26:3

PROVISION

Lord, I pray that you would give *(your husband's name)* and I wisdom when dealing with the money you provide for us. Teach us to be good stewards of your resources and give us cheerful hearts when giving back to you. I thank you that you will supply all of our needs according to your riches in glory by Christ Jesus. Please continue to teach us both how to trust in your hand for provision, not our own, because we know that it all belongs to you.

My God shall supply all your needs
according to His riches in glory by Christ Jesus.
Philippians 4:19

_____

_____

_____

_____

_____

REST

Lord, I come to you with the desire to make rest and renewal a priority in my life. You tell me in your word that you make me lie down in green pastures, you lead me beside quiet waters and you restore my soul, but I'm not living that kind of life. Most days I am running on less than empty, with no hope for rest in sight. Teach me today to follow you, my Good Shepherd. I submit to you my schedule, my to-do list and every other way that I try to control my day. Please make clear to me the way to my green pastures and quiet waters, and give me the discipline to remain in these places of rest until you restore my soul. Thank you for being a God that cares deeply about my need for rest and promises to always meet me in my quiet places.

The Lord is my shepherd, I shall not be in want. He makes me lie down in green pastures, he leads me beside quiet waters, he restores my soul....
Psalm 23:1-3

PATIENCE

Father, as a mom, there isn't a day that goes by that my patience isn't tried. Most days I fall flat on my face—patience lost before the clock strikes noon. So today I will cling to the promise that you will show patience to my precious little ones through me. Put my day into perspective, enable me to lighten up, and love them through me, I pray.

But the fruit of the Spirit is….patience.
Galatians 5:22

_____

_____

_____

_____

_____

PURPOSE

Father God, thank you that I can find my purpose clearly written in your Word: to know you and make you known (specifically to my children). I acknowledge today that I can't introduce you in an authentic way to my kids without knowing you authentically first. So, I pray that you would fan a flame in my heart for you. Make your Word come alive to me more than ever before, fix your words in my heart and mind, and change me from the inside out, I pray.

Fix these words of mine in your hearts and minds; tie them as symbols on your hands and bind them on your foreheads. Teach them to your children, talking about them when you sit at home and when you walk along the road, when you lie down and when you get up.
Deuteronomy 11:18-19

_____

_____

_____

_____

HUMILITY

Father God, infuse this pledge in my heart: I will do nothing out of selfish ambition or vain conceit, but in humility, I will consider my husband better than myself. Humble me to look not only at my own interests, but to his interests as well. Change my heart to accept that your way of humility and service is better than my shallow, selfish ways. I choose to trust you today!

Do nothing out of selfish ambition or vain conceit, but in humility consider others better than yourselves.
Each of you should look not only to your own interests, but also to the interests of others.
Philippians 2:3-4

_____

_____

_____

_____

_____

LOVE

Jesus, I fall short when it comes to loving my family the way you call me to love. The only love I can muster on my own is conditional, performance, appearance based love. I love when it's easy and convenient. Would you instead grow in me the fruit of unconditional love? Open the eyes of my heart so that I can begin to see my family as you do, and love them purely through me, I pray.

But the fruit of the Spirit is love.
Galatians 5:22

_____

_____

_____

_____

_____

HYPOCRISY

Father God, please expose any form of hypocrisy that may be found in my life. I pray that my relationship with you is more than just a form of lip service. Ignite a flame in my heart that burns with a genuine passion for you. Challenge me to continually maintain a walk that reflects my talk so that others are drawn to the true nature of you.

The Lord says, "These people come near to me with their mouth and honor me with their lips, but their hearts are far from me. Their worship of me is made up only of rules taught by men."
Isaiah 29:13

_____

_____

_____

_____

_____

PRIDE

Lord, forgive me for allowing pride to rear its ugly head in my life. I don't want to live in opposition to you, to be resisted, defeated or frustrated by you. Humility doesn't come naturally to me—my flesh actually loves to think that the world is all about me. However, today I will choose to clothe myself with humility. Fill me with your grace, I pray, so that I can follow wholeheartedly after you.

...all of you, clothe yourselves with humility toward one another, for God is opposed to the proud but gives grace to the humble.
1 Peter 5:5

_____

_____

_____

_____

_____

FREEDOM

Father God, thank you for the freedom that Jesus purchased for me through his death and resurrection. Forgive me for living in a way that suggests that I've forgotten that I've been set free. Will you show me how I have returned back to that enslaved way of thinking and living? Maybe it's not the big things anymore that imprison me but a host of little things, like tiny masters, that quietly keep me in chains. By your Spirit, please reveal these little masters for what they are so that I can put them back in their place.

It is for freedom that Christ has set us free.
Stand firm, then, and do not let yourselves
be burdened again by a yoke of slavery.
Galatians 5:1

MAKING HOME A SANCTUARY

Father God, I pray today that you would show me creative ways to make my home a sanctuary for my family—a place where they can find comfort and rest. I thank you that as we abide with you each day, you are among us—as an invisible guest at every meal and a silent listener to every conversation. Open our eyes to your presence each day, Lord, so we might learn to live in the midst of your glory.

I love the house where you live,
O Lord, the place where your glory dwells.
Psalm 26:8

_____

_____

_____

_____

_____

JOY

Father God, I pray I can hold fast to the cry, "the joy of the Lord is my strength". Remind me all throughout the day to look beyond those fleeting moments of happiness and rest in your infallible joy. Thank you that when I experience the joy only found in you, you will give me supernatural strength to press on through my day.

...for the joy of the Lord is your strength.
Nehemiah 8:10

ENERGY

Lord Jesus, I come to you today worn out, but full of hope! Thank you for reminding me that whatever the work may be, if you are not in it, it is meaningless. I pray today that you would expose the areas in my life where I am burning energy in vain. Refocus my perspective as I hold fast to you, and I will walk with confidence as you redeem my day!

Unless the Lord builds the house, its builders labor in vain.
Unless the Lord watches over the city,
the watchmen stand guard in vain.
Psalm 127:1

_____

_____

_____

_____

_____

THOUGHTS

Heavenly Father, thank you for giving me an amazing picture of what kind of thoughts are pleasing to you. I pray as I go about my day that you would teach me how to fix my mind on things that are true, noble and right—on things that are pure, lovely and admirable—on anything that is excellent and praiseworthy. Give me discipline to yield my thought life to you as my mind is renewed by the power of your Living Word.

Finally, brothers, whatever is true, whatever is noble, whatever is right, whatever is pure, whatever is lovely, whatever is admirable—if anything is excellent or praiseworthy—think about such things.
Philippians 4:8

TOPIC INDEX

ABOUT THE AUTHOR

Carrie Rogers is passionate about God's Word and its practical impact on the lives of women. She is the founder of Carried Away Ministries which seeks to encourage women to engage in a passionate pursuit of Jesus. Her two Bible studies, *The Wardrobe of Christ: Putting on the Character of Jesus* and *He Is …: Knowing God by Name* are available on Amazon. Carrie and her husband, Erik, along with their three children, reside in McKinney, Texas.

www.carriedawayministries.com

Made in the USA
Middletown, DE
02 August 2016